Reading American History

From Slavery to Freedom

Written by Melinda Lilly
Illustrated by Lori McElrath-Eslick

Educational Consultants
Kimberly Weiner, Ed.D
Betty Carter, Ed.D
Bill Garner, Los Angeles
Unified School District

Rourke
Publishing LLC
Vero Beach, Florida 32963

www.rourkepublishing.com

To Sarah Conterez, our grandmother,
Your love and patience have helped many people down the path to freedom.
—L. M.-E.

Designer: Elizabeth J. Bender

Library of Congress Cataloging-in-Publication Data

Lilly, Melinda.
   From slavery to freedom / Melinda Lilly; illustrated by Lori McElrath-Eslick.
      p. cm. — (Reading American history)
   Summary: Introduces the Underground Railroad, a group of people and places through which runaway slaves escaped to freedom before the Civil War.
   ISBN 1-58952-363-6
   1. Underground railroad—Juvenile literature. 2. Fugitive slaves—United States—Juvenile literature. [1. Underground railroad. 2. Fugitive slaves.] I. Eslick, illus. II. Title.

E450 .L59 2002
973.7'115—dc21   2002017845

Cover Illustration: Harriet Tubman leads an escaping slave to freedom.

Printed in the USA

Time Line

Help students follow this story by introducing important events in the Time Line.

1793   In the U. S., it is against the law to try to stop runaway slaves from being captured.

1849   Harriet Tubman escapes from slavery in Maryland.

1861   Beginning of the Civil War

1863   President Abraham Lincoln declares that slaves in the South are free.

1865   End of the Civil War

1865   The 13th Amendment to the U.S. Constitution makes slavery against the law.

Before 1865, many **African Americans** were slaves.

Slaves pick the crops.

The slaves wanted to be free.

Many ran away.

A slave runs away.

Some people helped slaves hide.
These people were called the
Underground Railroad.
The name explains that this was a
secret way to lead slaves to **freedom**.

Hiding in a hay cart

Runaway slaves and the people who helped them had to be brave. Slave catchers hunted them.

Hiding from a slave catcher

Freedom was far away.

The slave catcher's gun was close.

A slave catcher

The people of the Underground
Railroad looked for safe paths.

On a safe path

Free at last!

The long trip was over.

In this land, all African Americans
were free.

The runaway slaves are safe.

Some came back to help with the Underground Railroad.

Helping with the Underground Railroad

Harriet Tubman did!

She helped more than 300 people go from **slavery** to freedom.

Harriet Tubman

Word List

African Americans (AF rih ken uh MER ih kunz)—Americans of African descent

freedom (FREE dum)—The power to act as one chooses

runaway (RUN uh way)—A person who runs away

slavery (SLAY vuh ree)—The condition of being owned and controlled by a master

Tubman, Harriet (TUB mun, HAR ee et)—Harriet Tubman was a leader of the Underground Railroad and a former slave.

Underground Railroad (UN der ground RALE rode)—A way of helping runaway slaves escape to Canada or other lands where they could be free

Books to Read

Gayle, Sharon Shavers. *Escape!* Soundprints Corp. Audio, 1999.

Isaacs, Sally Senzell. *Life on the Underground Railroad.* Heinemann Library, 2001.

Kulling, Monica. *Escape North!: The Story of Harriet Tubman.* Random House, 2000.

Lutz, Norma Jean. *Harriet Tubman: Leader of the Underground Railroad.* Chelsea House Publishing, 2001.

Websites to Visit

www.nationalgeographic.com/railroad/j1.html

www.ciaccess.com/~jdnewby/museum.htm

http://blackhistorypages.com/Slavery/

www.germantown.k12.il.us/html/RAILROAD.html

www.cr.nps.gov/aahistory/ugrr/ugrr.htm

Index